Karen Marie Iversen

Modern
Bobbin Lace

Akacia

We have discovered that some of our customers have difficulties finding the Lurex thread. Therefore Karen Marie has made a list of substitution threads.

You can find the list on our homepage www.akacia.dk

Modern Bobbin Lace
By Karen Marie Iversen

© 2006 Forlaget Akacia
Skovvænget 1
5690 Tommerup
Denmark
akacia@akacia.dk

Printed at Økotryk I/S, Videbæk, Denmark, 2006

ISBN: 87-7847-091-9
ISBN-13: 978-87-7847-091-1

Preface

Right from childhood I have loved to doodle on a piece of paper – the curved lines fascinated me and one pattern inspired the next.

Back in 1993 I learned lace making, and at the same time I took painting classes at Mogens Noergaard. Even in the early days of my lace making I started to convert my water colour paintings into lace. I filled the various surfaces in the paintings with different grounds, 'painted' with beautiful colours in lace threads. As time went by, my doodles developed into lace patterns, useful for outfits and accessories and suitable for framing.

For this book I have made 18 designs and converted them into free lace. Some techniques are taken from Milanese and Duchesse lace.

Even though we talk about 'free lace', all designs are worked out with detailed drawings, diagrams and prickings, so no-one need to worry about having a go – the book will help you step by step.
Throughout the process, from the doodles to the finished patterns, my friend Bibi Tolstorf has been a great help. Without her constructive judgement and accuracy during the lace making, this book would not exist.
For that I am truly thankful.

My intention with this book is to show, that in the world of lace making you do not have to follow traditional thinking – you can make your own personal patterns based on your own ideas. Just have a go at free lace – it is not only fun but will take you forward.

Karen Marie Iversen
Greve, April 2006

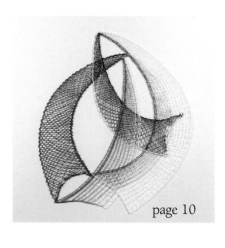

page 10

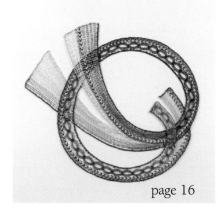

page 16

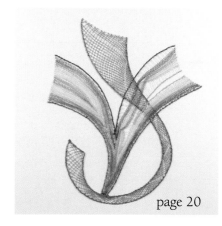

page 20

page 24

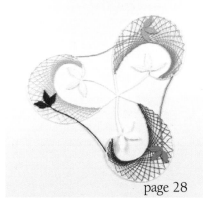

page 28

page 32

page 36

page 40

page 44

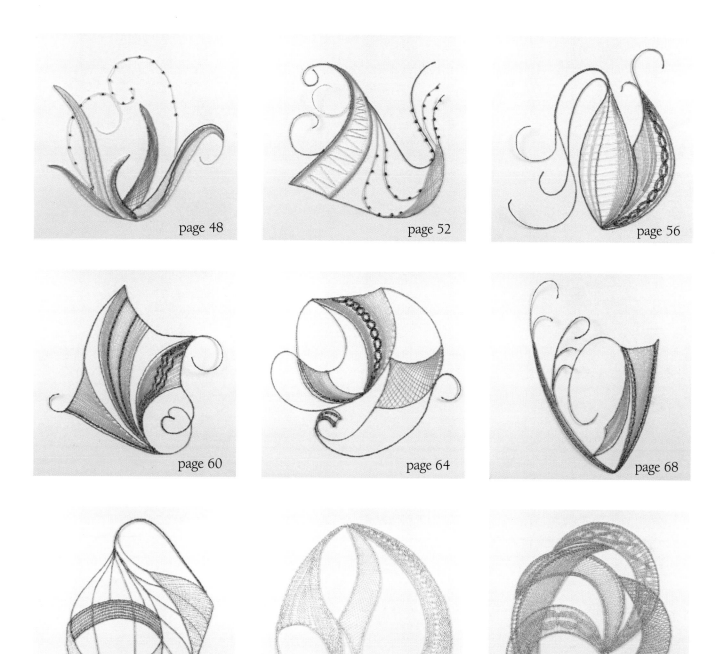

page 48

page 52

page 56

page 60

page 64

page 68

page 72

page 76

page 80

A few words about how to work the lace patterns

By working 'free lace' you are not tied to a sequence of working, there is no set spacing of pinholes or specific weight of thread – no rules at all.

In 'free lace' you start by drawing the outline of the motif you want to make in lace, then let your imagination guide you!

As you work, you decide how compact you want the lace (i.e. where you want to place the pinholes), you choose your work sequence/your pattern and you select your thread according to colour and weight.

All the motifs in this book have begun with an outline! And then I just enjoyed making the lace!
I have used techniques from Duchesse lace and braids from Milanese lace.

In Duchesse lace you make small designs, which finally are assembled into bigger designs linked with plaits. Milanese lace consists of braid lace with various grounds. The tapes are not supposed to cross each other, but sewings are used to join the work in progress.

In most of the motifs the workers are translucent Lurex thread. This thread has been chosen to set off the pattern in Milanese braid, and thus make the background "invisible".

Various types of plaits are used to connect the different motifs, with beads and glittery threads inserted in between. The desired result will appear after several trails, where different grounds, thread types, and techniques have been tested – only then can the actual pattern be designed.

The final work must be treated with starch (from Kantcentrum in Belgium).

1. Gimp in chain stitch

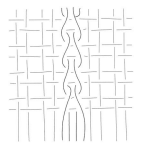

Lift bobbins 2 and 3, pass workers through and place bobbins 2 and 3 respectively to the left and right of bobbins 1 and 4.

2. Gimp with twist

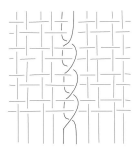

Lift bobbin 2 in the gimp and pass workers through. Place bobbin 2 to the left of bobbin 1.

3. Duchesse rolled edge

Gather all the bobbins in a bundle. Pick out one bobbin and make buttonhole stitches around the bundle.

4. Rib with four pairs and footside on the left

Start with whole stitch. Turn without using a pin and work back with the second pair from the right.

5. Venetian plait (little princess)

Twist both pairs and put bobbin 2 over bobbin 3. Pull up and repeat as many times as necessary.

6. Insert a new pair into a plait

Work to pinhole. Add one pair on the pin, make a whole stitch with this pair and continue the plait.

7. Linking two plaits

Pair 2 from the left plait and pair 1 from the right plait are joined with a turning stitch (double whole stich).

8. Linking a plait with a motif

Pair 2 from the plait joins with the motif by working a turning stitch (double whole stitch).

9. Windmill crossing with a gimp

Use one pair as one bobbin. Make a half stitch, put the gimp in the middle and cross "bobbins" 2 and 3.

10. Joining two plaits and two pairs

Using each pair from the plaits as a single bobbin, work whole stitch with the first plait from the left, put the gimp through and twist. Work a whole stitch with the two plaits, put the gimp through and work whole stitch with the worker.

11. Sewing into the lower bar on the edge

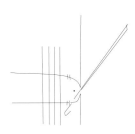

A bar is where the workers are twisted together between the passive pairs and the edge pair. The drawing shows sewing into the lower bar.

12. Tally/leaf worked with plait on the reverse side

Make the leaf. Turn the lace pillow 180 degrees and take the pairs around the pin. Work back over top of the leaf and sew in the pairs.

13. Mounting bead between two pieces of clothwork

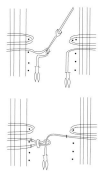

Attach a bead to a hook. Pull the worker from the left hand side through the bead, pass the worker from the right hand side through the loop and tighten up.

14. Mounting bead in a plait

Attach a bead to a hook. Pull the thread from bobbin 4 through the bead, pass bobbin 3 through the loop and tighten up.

15. Joining onto plait with worker in whole stitch

Cross bobbin 4 in the plait and bobbin 1 of the whole stitch workers twice. Twist bobbin 4 and 3 in the plait. Twist the worker pair. Cross bobbin 3 in the plait with bobbin 2 of the workers twice.

16. Plait with four pairs

Use each pair as one bobbin. Twist, cross and tighten up as you go along.

Colour coding
Purple:...... whole stitch/cloth stitch
Red:.......... cloth stitch and twist
Green: ...... half stitch
Black: .... pinholes/twists/plaits/gimps

No. 1

Threads: Lurex 7005, worker
DMC 5287, grey metallic
DMC 5272, frosted white
Venus 675, purple
Venus 673, lilac
Anchor 301 – 2 strands, silver
Venus 900, black

Fig. 1:
Start with one pair of purple for the straight edge on the left hand side, two pairs of purple for the plait across the motif and one pair of Lurex for the worker. The plait starts as follows:
pins 2 and 3: one pair, purple
pins 4 – 7: one pair, lilac
pins 8 – 10: one pair, frosted white
The threads are divided as follows:
Across pins 5 and 6 hang one pair of lilac and one pair of purple, so that each pair consists of both colours.
On pins 7 and 8 2-threads of lilac form a passive pair.
On pin 9 and 10, 1 thread lilac and 1 thread frosted white form a passive pair. The last two pairs continues as a plait at right hand side.
Work according to the diagram and leave out pairs as shown. 2 pairs of purple and the worker are carried on to fig.2

Fig. 2:
The two purple pairs follow the left hand side, as shown in the diagram. Add nine pairs of grey metallic according to the diagram. Finish off all pairs with a plait at the end of the motif.

Starch the work twice before removing from the lace pillow.

Fig. 3:
On pin 1 hang one pair of grey metallic, two pairs of frosted white for the plait going across the motif and one pair of Lurex the worker. Add the following pairs in this sequence from left to right: one pair of grey metallic, six pairs of silver, and six pairs of frosted white.
The plait continues on the right hand side of the motif. Work according to the diagram, and leave out pairs as shown.
The Lurex worker, two pairs of frosted white and two pairs of grey metallic are carried on to fig. 4.

Fig. 4:
On pin 1 hang one pair of black for the straight edge on the left hand side, and the two pairs of frosted white continue as a plait on the right hand side. Five pairs of purple are added as shown. Finish off with a plait.

Starch the work twice before removing from the lace pillow.

Sew the two motifs together.

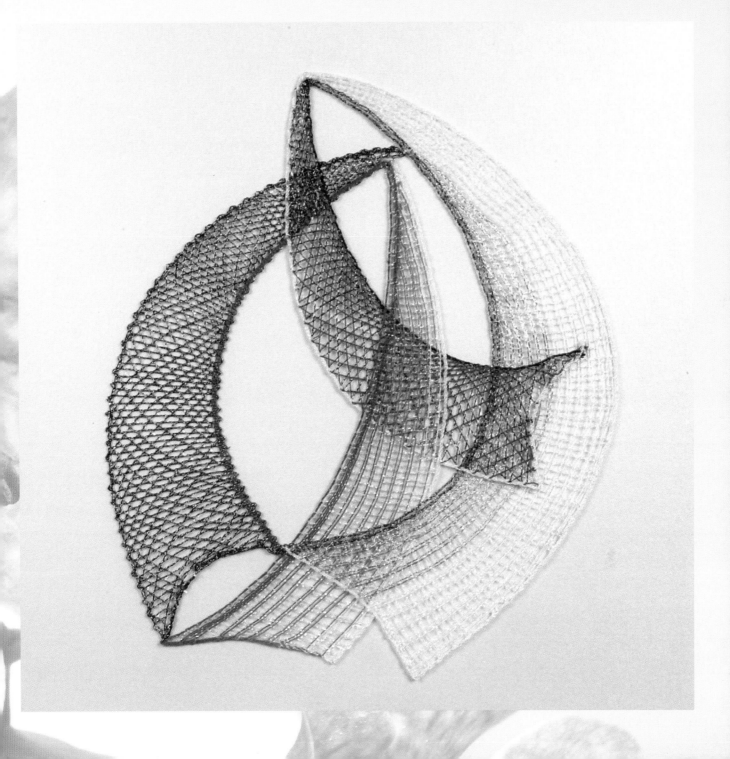

Diagram

fig. 1

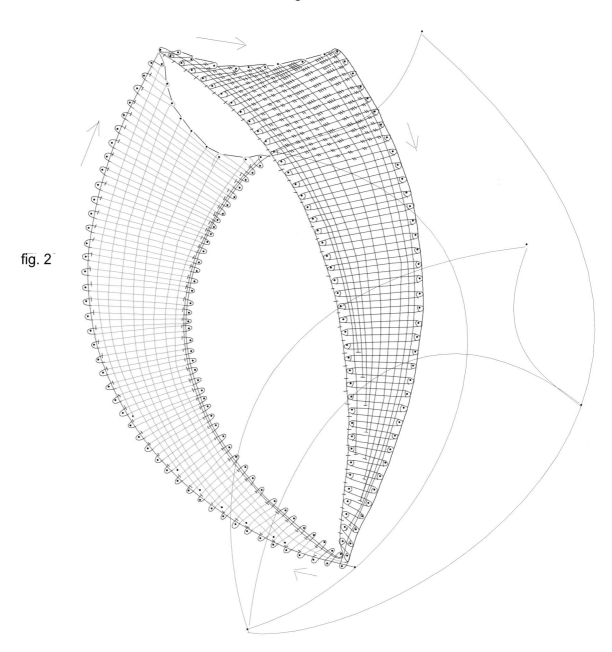

fig. 2

Diagram

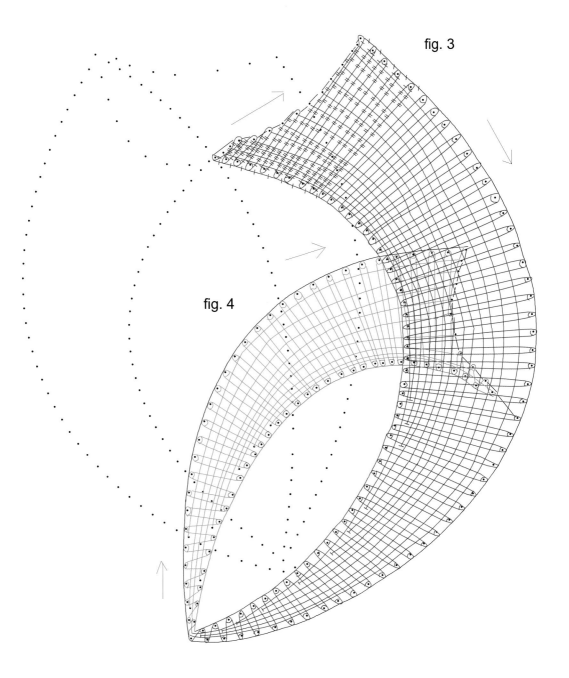

fig. 3

fig. 4

Pricking

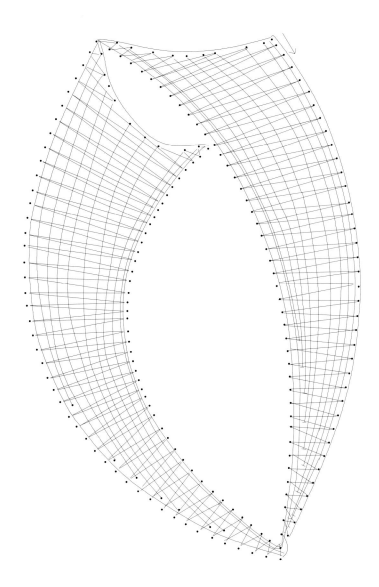

Pricking

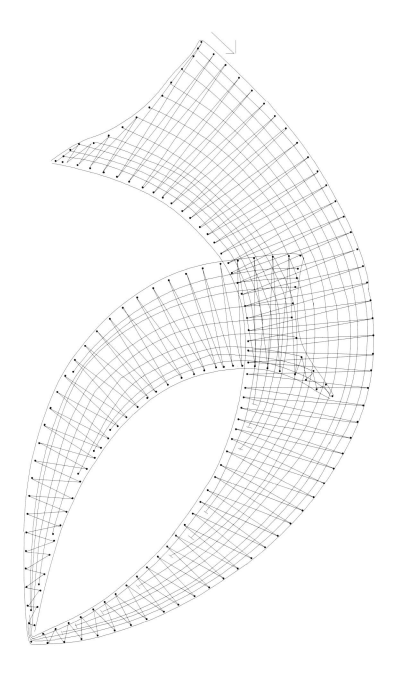

No. 2

Threads: Lurex 7005, worker
DMC 5287, grey metallic
DMC 5272, frosted white
DMC 52, variegated violet, please see below
Venus 500, dark purple
Venus 673, lilac
Venus 678, pale lilac
Anchor 108, light lavender
Anchor 96, light violet
Venus 499, cerise
Venus 108, light cerise

Variegated violet: find the darkest section of the thread, fold here and wind the bobbins.

Fig. 1:
On pin 1 hang two pairs of variegated violet for the edge plait on the left hand side, two pairs of pale lilac for the plait across the motif, and one pair of Lurex for the worker. Add the pairs in the plait across the motif in the following sequence: four pairs of variegated violet, two gimp pairs for chain stitch, please see technique drawing No. 1 on page 7, consisting of one pair of grey metallic and one pair of frosted white and finally one pair of variegated violet. Now the plait will change colour because the new pairs plait to the next pin, and the "old" pairs from the plait continue as passive pairs in the motif.
Add the new pairs in this sequence: on pin 7 one pair of light cerise, which goes into the plait, one pair of pale lilac used as passive pair.
On pin 8 one pair of light cerise and the last pair of pale lilac are used as passive pairs.
The plait is now light cerise. From the last two pins the light cerise disappears down into the work. The right hand side is made with turning stitch.
Continue the work to the point, where it meets with fig. 2.

Fig. 2:
Add pairs in the following sequence from the right: two pairs of variegated violet for the edge plait and two pairs of pale cerise for plait across the motif.
In the plait add pairs as in fig. 1 in the following sequence: one pair of dark purple, two pairs of pale lilac, two pairs of light lavender, two pairs of light violet, and four pairs of pale lilac.
The two pairs of light cerise from the plait become passive pairs on the last two pins.
On the last pin add one pair of Lurex for the worker.
Continue according to the diagram until point A.
Point A:
Add pairs in the following sequence:
one pair of lilac, follow the tape to the left,
two pairs of light cerise, follow the tape to the right,
one pair of Lurex worker for the left tape,
one pair of dark purple, follow the tape to the left,
one pair of pale lilac, follow the tape to the right,
three pairs of pale lilac, follow the tape to the right.
The pairs end up in the plaits on the two tapes.

Starch the work twice before finishing off and removing from the lace pillow.

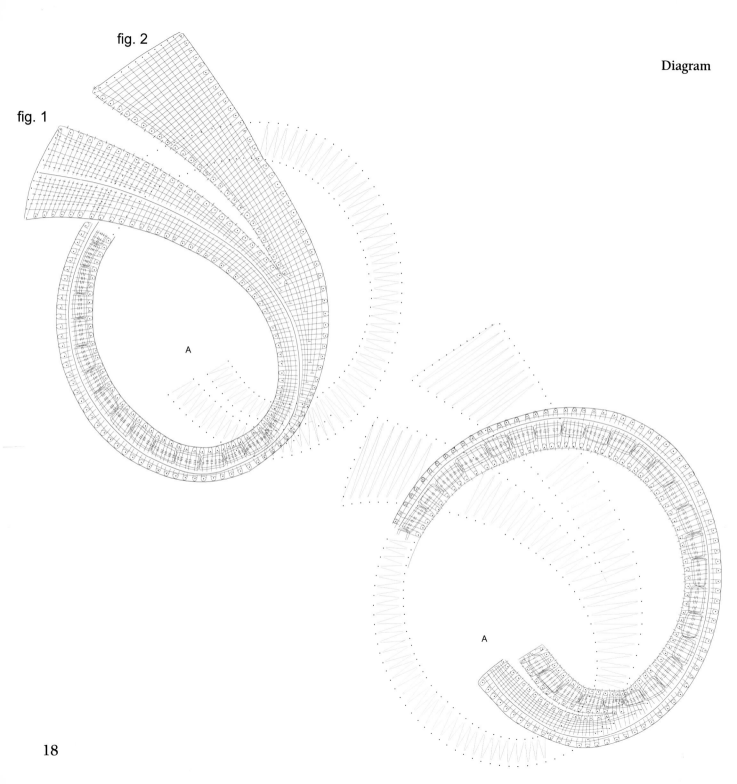

fig. 2

fig. 1

Diagram

A

A

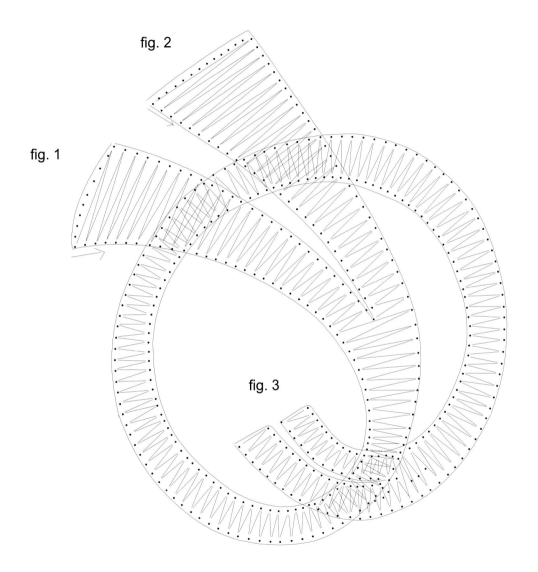

fig. 1

fig. 2

fig. 3

No. 3

Threads: Lurex 7005, worker
DMC 5287, grey metallic
DMC 52, variegated violet, please see below
Venus 500, dark purple   Venus 673, lilac
Venus 678, pale lilac   Anchor 108, light lavender
Venus 499, cerise   Venus 108, light cerise

Variegated violet: find the darkest section of the thread, fold here and wind the bobbins.

Fig. 1:
Start on the left hand side. Add two pairs of grey metallic for the edge plait at the left hand side of the motif and two pairs of Lurex for the plait going across the motif.
To the Lurex plait add twelve pairs of lilac as shown by the markings, and two pairs of grey metallic for the edge plait on the right hand side.
One Lurex pair is left out of the work from pin 1 on the right hand side. The other Lurex pair from the plait continues as the worker.
Pins 4 and 6 from the right hand side at the top of motif are to be reused (lift the pins and put them back again). Remember one twist at each turning stitch on both sides to keep the Lurex thread as a worker (half stitch). Continue according to the diagram, and leave the pairs out as shown. Finish off all pairs with a plait.
Starch the work twice before removing from the lace pillow.

Fig. 2A:
Start on the right hand side by adding two pairs of cerise for the edge plait on the right hand side, and two pairs of Lurex for the plait going across the motif.
In this plait add pairs in the following sequence:
two pairs of pale lilac, two pairs of light lavender, two pairs of lilac, two pairs of variegated violet, and two pairs of grey metallic for the edge plait on the left hand side.
One Lurex pair from the plait is left out of the work, the other Lurex pair continues as worker.
Pins 2 and 4 from the left hand side at the top of motif are to be reused. Continue according to the diagram, and leave the pairs out as shown. Leave aside the pairs at the point, where fig. 2A and 2B meet.

Fig 2B:
Start on the left hand side with two pairs of cerise for the edge plait on the left hand side, and two pairs of Lurex for the plait across the motif.
Add pairs in this plait in the following sequence:
one pair of light cerise, one pair of pale lilac, one pair of light lavender, two pairs of lilac, two pairs of dark purple, and two pairs of variegated violet for the edge plait on the right hand side. Continue according to the diagram.
At the point where fig. 2A and 2B meet, leave out one Lurex worker pair and continue according to the diagram to the point, where fig. 3 joins.

Fig. 3:
Start on the right hand side with two pairs of grey metallic for the edge plait, and two pairs of Lurex for the plait across the motif.
Into this plait add pairs in the following sequence:
two pairs of dark purple, two pairs of lilac, two pairs of light lavender, two pairs of pale lilac, one pair of light cerise, three pairs of cerise, one pair of light cerise, two pairs of pale lilac, two pairs of light lavender, two pairs of lilac, two pairs of dark purple, and two pairs of variegated violet for the edge plait on the left hand side.
One pair of Lurex from the plait is left out, and the other pair continues as the worker.
Pins 3 and 8 from the left hand side at the top of the motif are to be reused. Continue and fasten off at the end of the diagram.

Starch the work twice before removing from the lace pillow. Sew the two motifs together.

fig. 2 A

fig. 2 B

Diagram

fig. 3

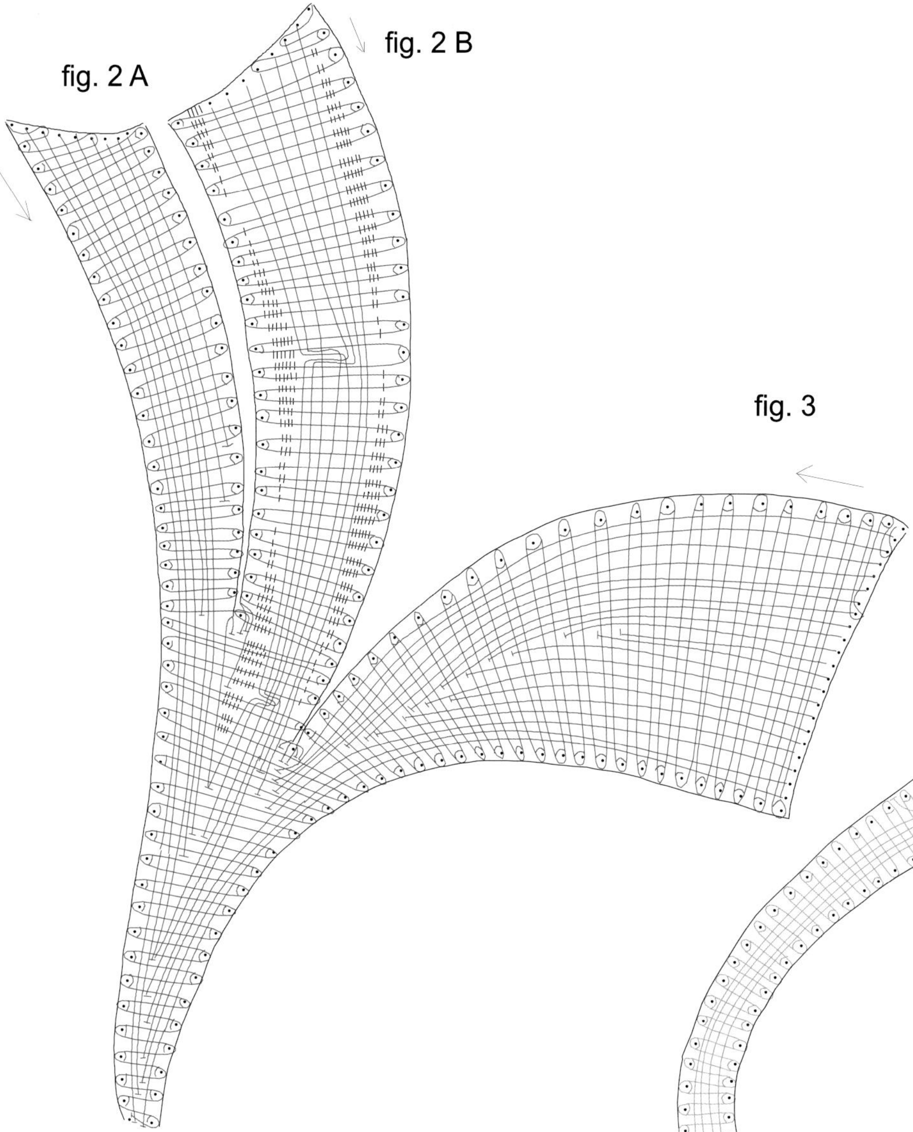

fig. 1

22

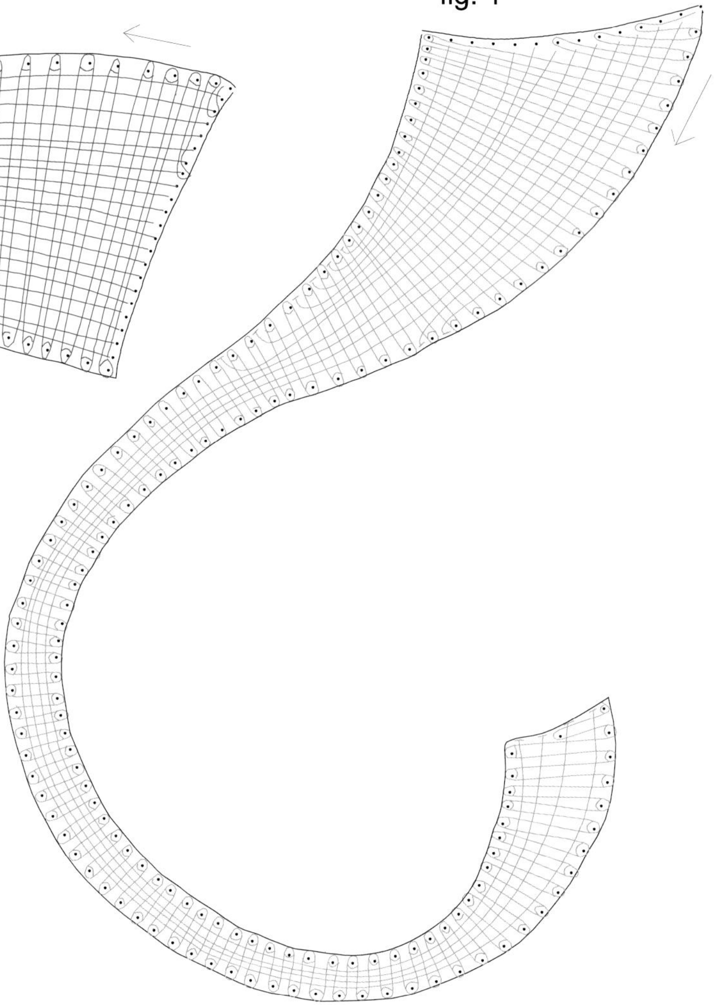

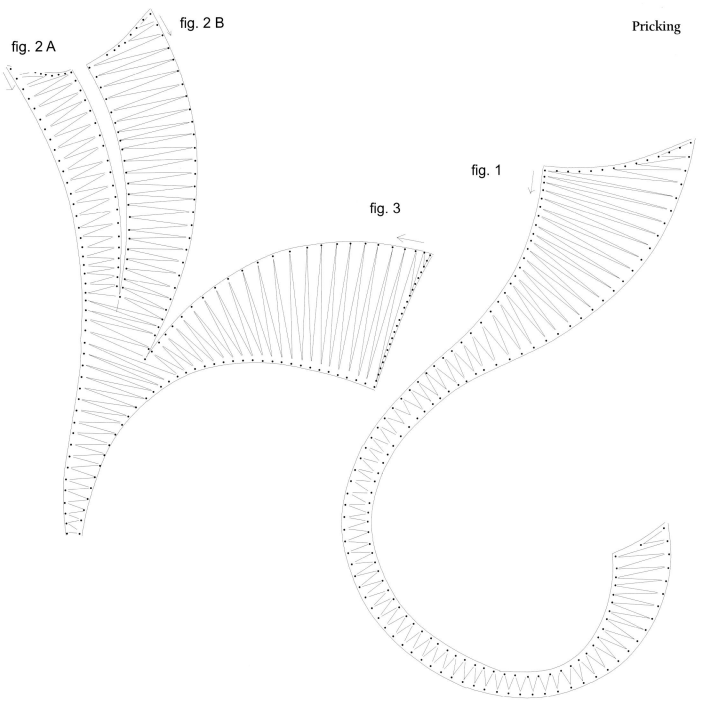

fig. 2 A

fig. 2 B

fig. 3

fig. 1

Pricking

23

No. 4

Threads: Lurex 7005, worker
Venus 191, bordeaux
DMC 99, variegated mauve, please see below
Mayflower 2213-2, light red
Venus 499, cerise

Variegated mauve1: find the darkest section of the thread, fold here and wind the bobbins.
Variegated mauve2: find the lightest section of the thread, fold here and wind the bobbins.

Point A:
Start with two pairs of bordeaux and two pairs of variegated mauve1 for a rib, please see technique drawing No. 4 on page 7. Work the rib to the start of the diagram.
The two pairs of bordeaux continue as a plait on the left hand side of the motif, the two pairs of variegated mauve1 continues as passive pairs.
On pin 1 add one Lurex worker and one more pair of variegated mauve1. Continue to the point where the work from Point B joins. Leave the pairs aside.

Point B:
Start with two pairs of light red for the leaf stalk, work the leaf and plait back to the base of the leaf.
Continue to work the leaf stalk and leaves. The plait continues on the right hand side of the motif.
Add two pairs of variegated mauve1 for a plait across the motif and one Lurex worker.
Add pairs to the plait in the following sequence: two pairs of cerise and two pairs of bordeaux. The pairs from the plait are now used as passive pairs. Continue according to the diagram.
At the end of the motif the outer two pairs, closest to point D, continue to plait and form a leaf stalk.
Finish off all remaining pairs.

Point C:
Start with two pairs of variegated mauve2 for the leaf stalk. Work the plait and leaves. Sew in the pairs.

Point D:
Start with four pairs of Bordeaux for a rib, please see technique drawing No. 4 on page 7.
Into this rib, add pairs for the "ear" according to the colour sequence: one pair of Lurex for the worker, one pair of bordeaux, one pair of cerise, one pair of bordeaux, and two pairs of cerise for a plait on the right hand side.
Work according to the diagram, and finish off all pairs in the edge plait.
Finish the rib and sew in the pairs.

Starch the work twice before removing from the lace pillow.

Diagram

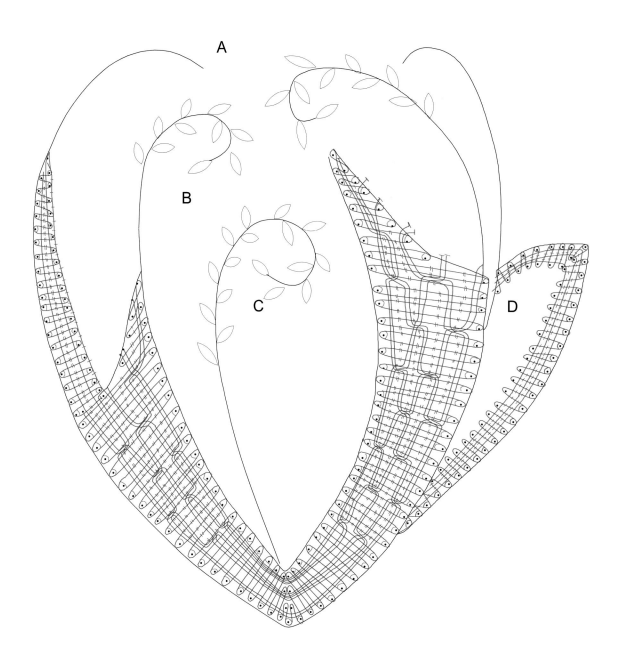

Pricking

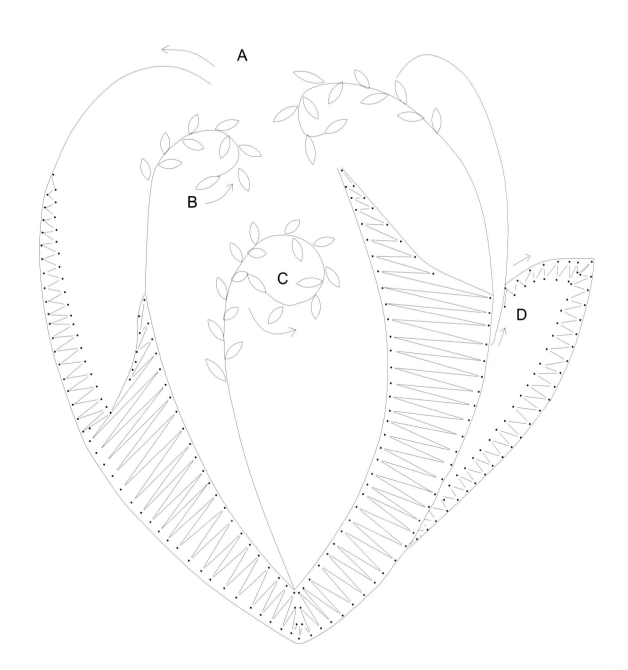

No. 5

Threads: Lurex 7005, worker
DMC 5272, frosted white
Venus 191, bordeaux
Venus 499, cerise
Venus 108, light cerise

Start making the leaves in fig. 1, 2, and 3.
Point A:
Make three leaves, and plait back when necessary with two pairs of bordeaux. Plait to the start of fig. 2. Leave the pairs aside.
Point B:
Make three leaves, and plait back when necessary with two pairs of cerise. Plait to the start of fig. 3. Leave the pairs aside.
Point C:
Make three leaves, and plait back when necessary with two pairs of light cerise. Plait to the start of fig. 1. Leave the pairs aside.
Point D:
Make three leaves, and plait back when necessary with two pairs of frosted white. Plait to the start of fig. 1.

Fig. 1:
Start with one Lurex worker and four pairs of cerise. The plaited pairs from point C continue as passive pairs in a Torchon ground (half stitch). Work across the bordeaux leaves according to the diagram. Remember one twist at the turning stitch on both sides to keep the Lurex worker together. Leave out pairs as shown in the diagram. The plait continues to point E. At this point the plait turns and continues according to the diagram.

Fig. 2 and 3:
To be made in the same way.
The colours in the Torchon ground are as follows:
fig. 1: Bordeaux leaves and light cerise ground.
fig. 2: Light cerise leaves and cerise ground.
fig. 3: Cerise leaves and bordeaux ground.

Sew in the third time the plait gets to point E.

Starch the work twice before removing from the lace pillow.

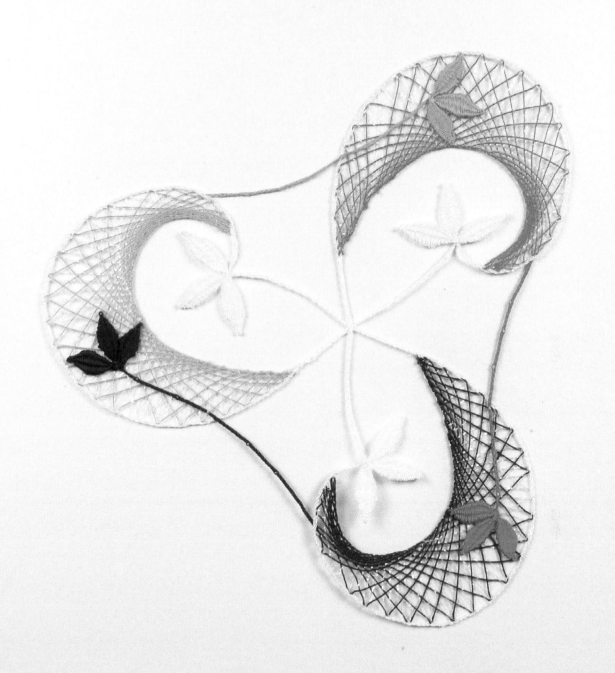

Diagram

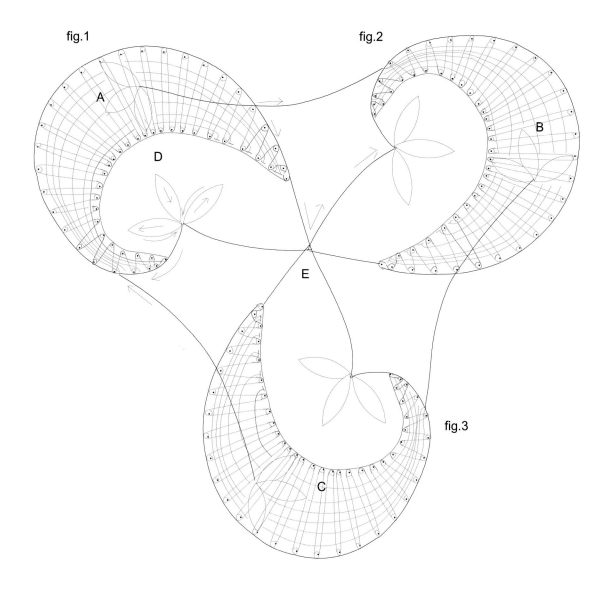

fig.1

fig.2

fig.3

A

B

C

D

E

Pricking

fig.2

fig.1

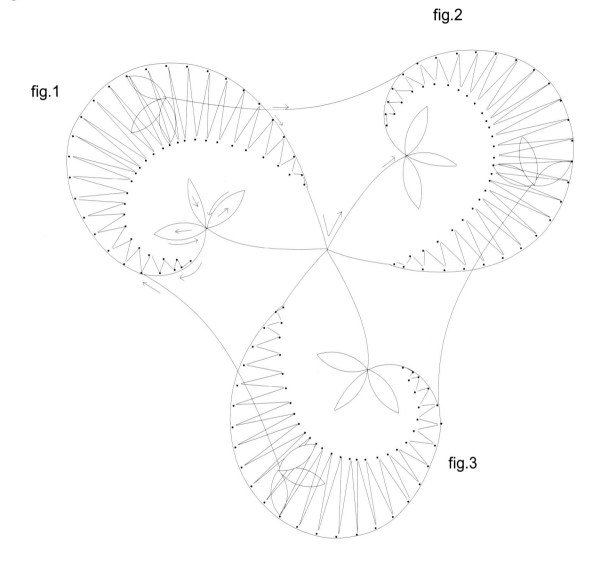

fig.3

31

No. 6

Threads: Lurex 7005, worker
DMC 99, variegated mauve, please see below
Venus 191, bordeaux
DMC 3687, mauve
Venus 105, light cerise
DMC 5200, frosted white
Madeira Metallic 5287, grey metallic

Variegated mauve: find the darkest section of the thread, fold here and wind the bobbins.

Points A and B:
Start with two pairs of variegated mauve on each leaf stalk and work down to fig. 1. (Plait back when necessary on the leaves).

Fig. 1:
Start with one Lurex worker pair. The pairs from the two leaf stalks continue as passive.
Add two pairs of bordeaux hung open, add one pair of Lurex for the worker as shown and follow the diagram. Leave out the pairs as shown in the diagram. Make the outer two pairs into a plait. (The plait is now more pale). Plait to the start of fig. 1. Sew in the plait and continue the plait to point D. Leave the pairs aside.

Point C:
Start with two pairs of light cerise for the leaf stalk and plait down to point D. The plaits are joined and continue as a Duchesse rolled edge to point E, please see technique drawing No. 3 on page 7.

Point E:
Two pairs of the light cerise continue from the Duchesse roll continues as a plait across fig. 2 and the other two pairs are to be used as the edge plait on the right hand side of the motif.

Fig. 2:
Add pairs to the plait in the following colour sequence: one Lurex worker, one pair of bordeaux, two pairs of frosted white, two pairs of light cerise, two pairs of bordeaux, one pair of mauve, one pair of bordeaux, one pair of grey metallic, one pair of bordeaux, one pair of mauve, three pairs of bordeaux, one pair of light cerise, and two pairs of frosted white. Follow the diagram.
The edge plaits join in a windmill crossing, please see technique drawing No. 9 on page 8. Fasten off the pairs.

Starch the work twice before removing from the lace pillow.

Arrange fig. 2 through fig. 1, and the tip of the funnel is stitched to the plait.

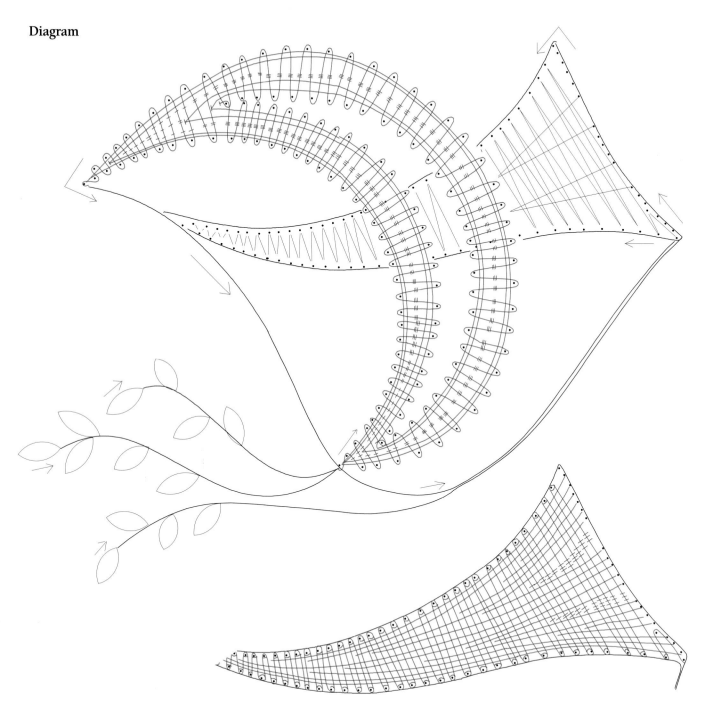

34

Pricking

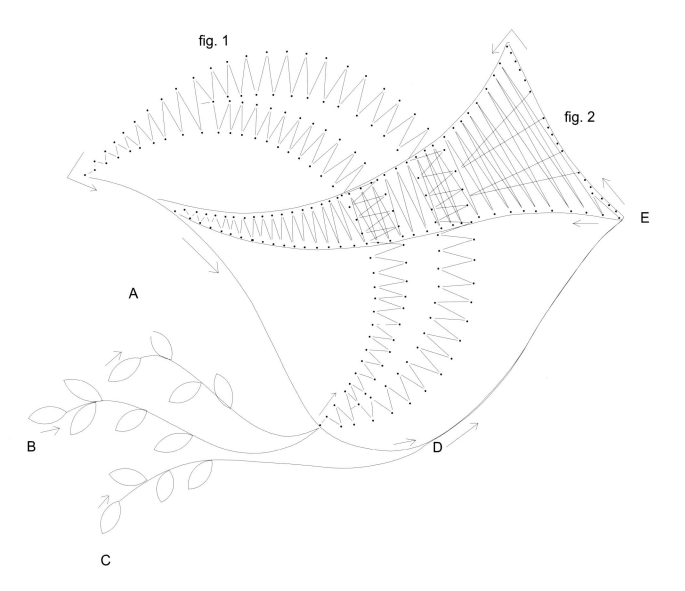

fig. 1

fig. 2

A

B

C

D

E

No. 7

Threads: Lurex 7005, worker
Anchor 320, undivided, as gimp
Venus 368, dark blue
DMC 798, medium delft blue
Anchor 248, pale blue
Beads: 3 mm

Fig. 1:
Start with two pairs of dark blue and two pairs of Lurex for the edge plaits on respectively left and right hand sides. Add one Lurex worker and three pairs of pale blue at the markings on the diagram.
When the next "tape" appears, add six pairs of medium delft blue according to the diagram.
At the start of "tape" 3 add one extra Lurex worker, four pairs of pale blue, and one gimp pair, please see technique drawing No. 2 on page 7. Follow the markings on the diagram.
The two "tapes" are made simultaneously and the third "tape" is worked into them with a whole stitch at the pins in the middle.
Leave out pairs according to the diagram.

Fig. 2:
Start with two pairs of dark blue and two pairs of pale blue for the edge plaits.
Add one Lurex worker and four pairs of medium delft blue at the markings on the diagram. Remember one twist at the turning stitch on both sides to keep the Lurex workers together.
Leave out pairs according to the diagram.
Finish off the last pairs in a Duchesse rolled edge, please see technique drawing No. 3 on page 7, and fasten the rolled edge to the motif.
Point A:
Start with two pairs of dark blue in a plait. Add fourteen white beads as shown on the diagram, please see technique drawing No. 14 on page 9.
Point B:
Start with two pairs of medium delft blue in a plait. Add twelve medium delft blue beads as shown on the diagram.
Point C:
Start with two pairs of pale blue in a plait. Add eight silver beads as shown on the diagram.

Starch the work twice before removing from the lace pillow.

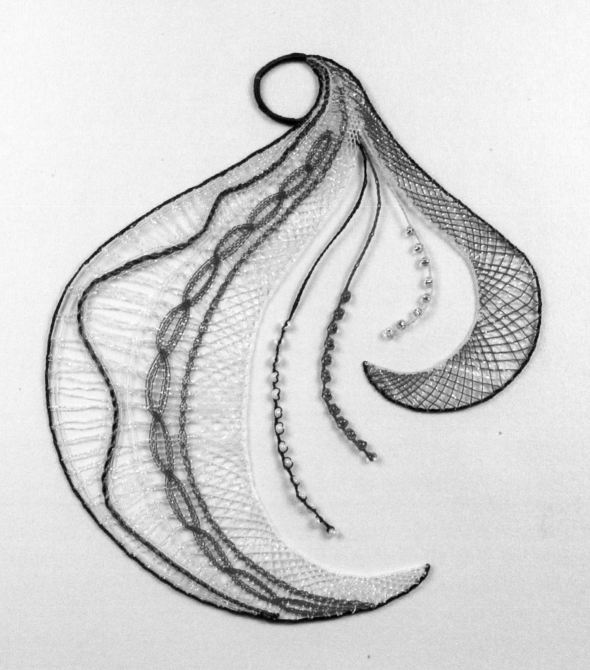

Diagram

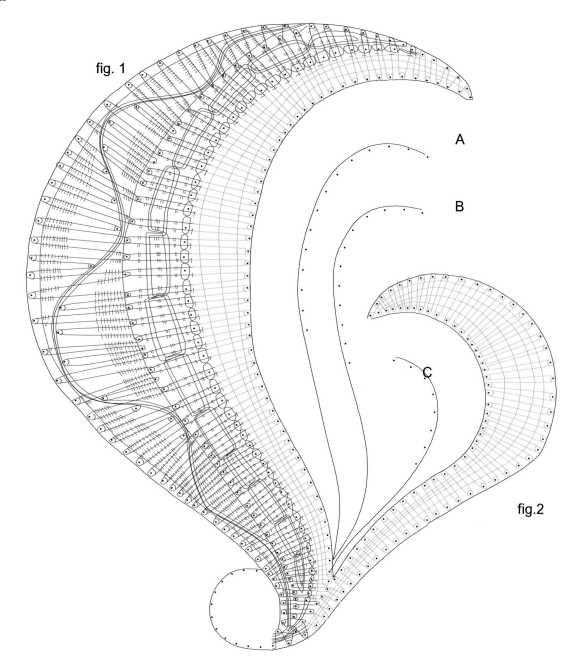

fig. 1

A

B

C

fig.2

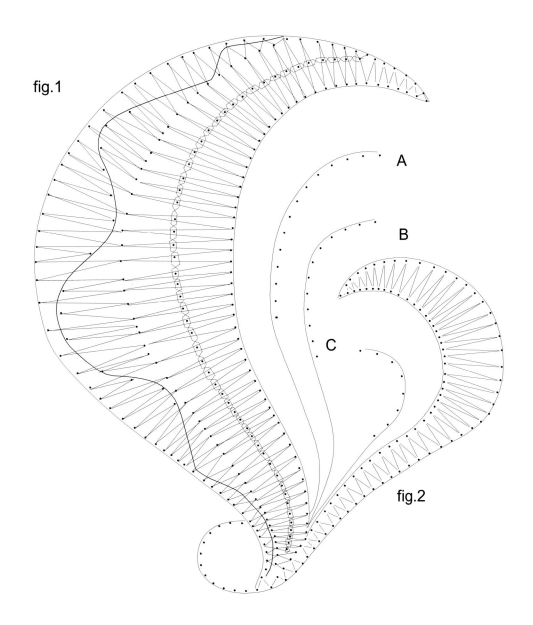

fig.1

fig.2

A

B

C

No. 8

Threads: Lurex 7005, worker
DMC 5287, grey metallic
Venus 368, dark blue
DMC 798, medium delft blue
Anchor 248, pale blue
Beads: 2 mm

Point A:
Start with two pairs of grey metallic for a plait on the left
hand side and one Lurex worker pair. Follow the diagram
and add in pairs in the following colour sequence.
two pairs of dark blue, two pairs of delft blue, two pairs
of pale blue, two pairs of dark blue, and two pairs of medium delft blue. Follow the diagram to point B.

Point B:
Add pairs in the following colour sequence at the markings:
two pairs of dark blue, two pairs of medium delft blue,
one pair of pale blue, and one Lurex worker pair. Work
according to the diagram and leave out pairs as shown.

Point C:
Start with two pairs of grey metallic and plait to the start
of the motif.
On pin 1 add one Lurex pair and then the following
colour sequence: one pair of medium delft blue, and two
pairs of dark blue. Follow the diagram and finish off in
the plait.

Plaits with beads and leaves:
Add two pairs of medium delft blue at the markings.
Make the leaves and plait back when necessary.
Add the beads, please see technique drawing No. 14 on
page 9, sew in the plaits and fasten them off.

Starch the work twice before removing from the lace pillow.

Diagram

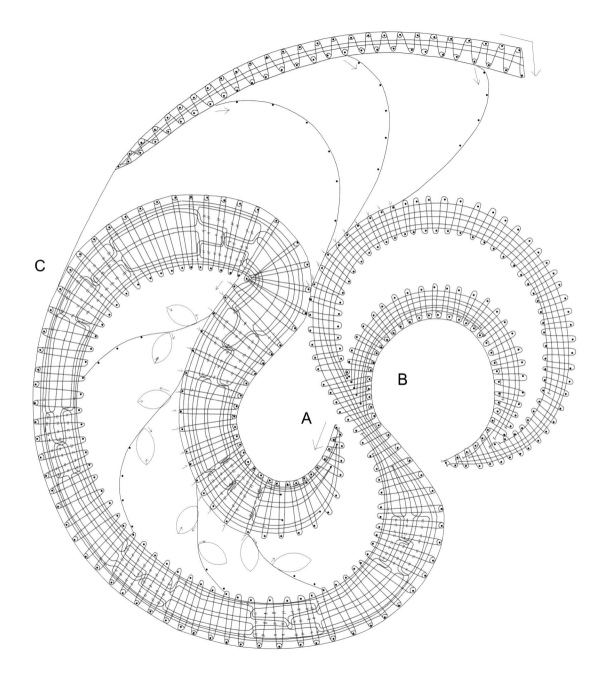

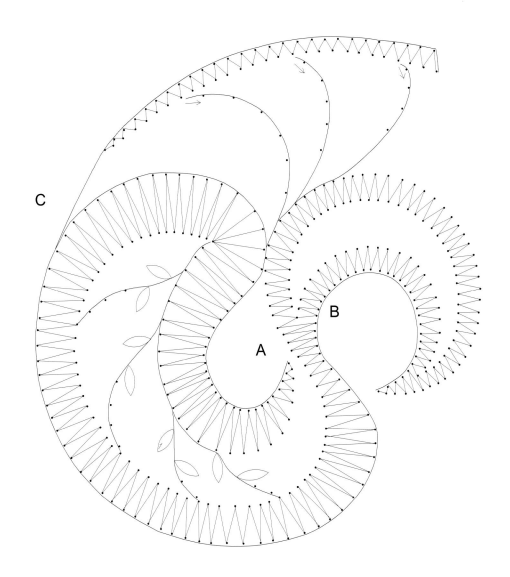

C

B

A

No. 9

Threads: Lurex 7005, worker
DMC 5283, silver, gimp
Venus 368, dark blue
DMC 798, medium delft blue
Venus 363, light blue
Anchor 248, pale blue

Fig. 1:
Start with two pairs of medium delft blue (left plait), two pairs of pale blue (right plait), and one Lurex worker.
In the left plait add pairs in the following colour sequence: three pairs of dark blue, one pair of pale blue, two pairs of light blue, two pairs of medium delft blue, and one pair of dark blue.
Work according to the diagram. At the end of the motif the plait continues to fig. 2.

Fig. 2:
Point A:
Start with two pairs of pale blue and plait to the point where A and B meet. Leave the pairs aside.
Point B:
Start with two pairs of light blue and plait to the point where B meets A. The pairs from the two plaits now work a rib, please see technique drawing No. 4 on page 7, continue the rib down to fig. 2.
The pale blue plait continues on the left hand side of the motif, and the light blue continues across the motif. Add pairs to the plait in the following colour sequence: one pair of dark blue, one pair of light blue, two pairs of medium delft blue, two pairs of dark blue, one pair of silver gimp, two pairs of dark blue, one pair medium of delft blue, one pair of light blue, and one pair of medium delft blue.
Continue according to the diagram to fig. 3.

Fig. 3:
The silver gimp, two pairs of medium delft blue, and the worker continue in fig. 3. Arrange one pair of medium delft blue and one pair of silver so that one silver thread and one blue thread form pairs on each side of the motif. Add one pair of pale blue when required. Continue according to the diagram.
Sew the plait into three pinholes along fig. 3 and continue to fig. 1. Sew in and fasten off.

Starch the work twice before removing from the lace pillow.

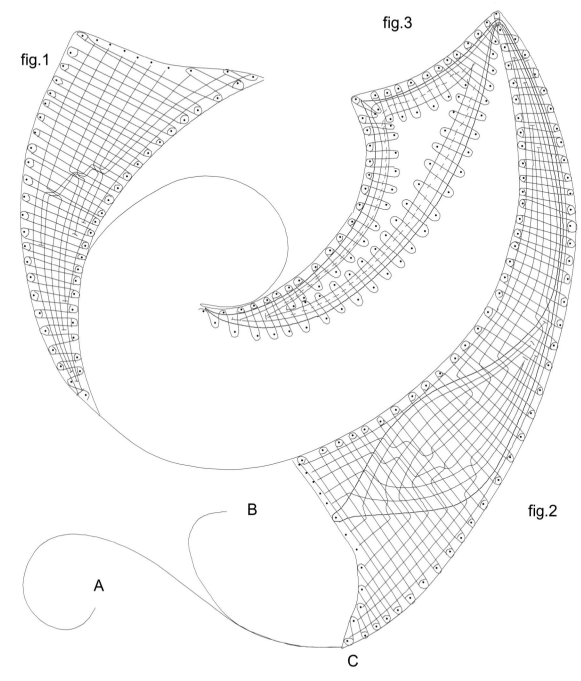

fig.1

fig.3

fig.2

A

B

C

Pricking

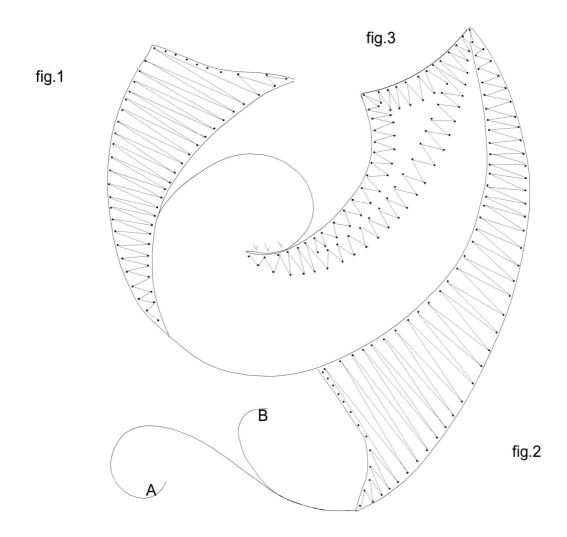

fig.1

fig.3

fig.2

A

B

No. 10

Threads: Lurex 7005, worker
DMC 5287, grey metallic
DMC 701, dark green
Venus 229, medium green
Anchor 240, light grass green
Anchor 259, light loden green
Beads: 2 mm

Leaf 1:
Start with two pairs of grey metallic on the first pin for the plait on the right hand side, and two pairs of medium green for the plait on the left hand side, plus one Lurex worker and two pairs of light loden green. Then add two pairs of light grass green and two pairs of light loden green, all according to the diagram.
Where the leaves meet, leave the pairs aside and start leaf 2.

Leaf 2:
Start with two pairs of dark grass green (plait) and one Lurex worker.
Add pairs according to the diagram in the following colour sequence: two pairs of light green and two pairs of medium green, work according to the diagram. Leaf 1 and leaf 2 are joined, continue to the point, where the work meets leaf 3.

Leaf 3:
Start with two pairs of dark green on pin 1 for the right hand side plait and two pairs of Lurex for plait on the right hand side and one Lurex worker.
Work according to the diagram and add pairs in the following colour sequence: one pair of dark grass green, one pair of medium green, and two pairs of light green. Before joining the three leaves the Lurex plait is to be left out.
Join the leaves and work to the point where the last two leaves join.

Leaf 4:
Start with two pairs of grey metallic on pin 1 for the right hand side plait and two pairs of medium green for the plait on the left hand side.
On the same pin add one Lurex worker and two pairs of medium green.
Work according to the diagram and add pairs in the following colour sequence: two pairs of medium green, three pairs of dark green, and work half stitch to the point where leaf 5 is to be added.

Leaf 5:
Point A:
Start with two pairs of light loden green for a plait. Add beads to the plait according to the diagram, please see technique drawing No. 14 on page 9. The pairs from this plait are carried as passive pairs in the leaf.
Point B:
Start with two pairs of dark grass green and plait to the tip. Hang two pairs of light green on pin 1 for the plait on the right hand side and one Lurex worker.
Add pairs in the following colour sequence: one pair of light grass green for the left hand side of the leaf, one pair of dark green for the right side of the leaf, two pairs of medium green, one pair of light loden green, one pair of dark green, and two pairs of light loden green.
Work according to the diagram. Join leaves 4 and 5, and finish off according to the diagram.
The last plait with beads is worked with two pairs of light loden green. Finish at the point where the plaits meet.

Starch the work twice before removing from the lace pillow.

Diagram

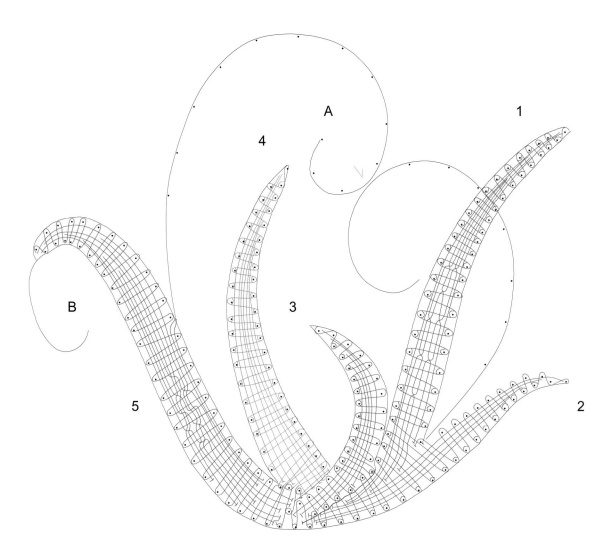

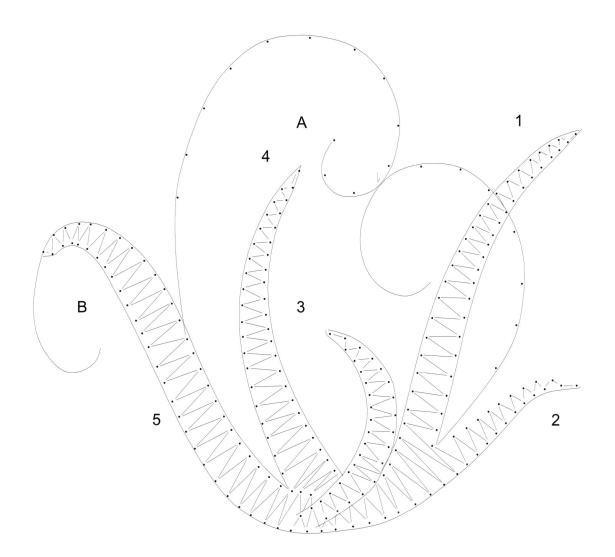

No. 11

Threads: Lurex 7005, worker
DMC 5287, grey metallic
DMC 5283, silver – using two out of six strands
DMC 701, dark green
Venus 229, medium green
Anchor 240, light grass green
Anchor 259, light loden green
Beads: 2 mm

Point 1:
Start with two pairs of grey metallic, plait to the motif.
Leave the pairs aside.

Point 2:
Start with two pairs of silver, plait to the motif. Leave the
pairs aside.

Point 3:
On pin 1 add four pairs of grey metallic for plaits (for left and
right hand sides). On the same pin add one Lurex worker.
From left to right on a lying pin add: one pair of dark
green, one pair of medium green, one pair of light grass
green, and one pair of light loden green.
Work in whole stitch according to the diagram. On pin
4 in this tape add two pairs of silver (two strands) for
a plait, which will zigzag between the tapes. Please see
technique drawing No. 8 on page 8.
For the other tape add one Lurex pair on the first pin and
work into the plait.
On a lying pin add pairs in the following colour sequence: one pair of light loden green, one pair of light
grass green, one pair of medium green, and one pair of
dark green. Continue according to the diagram. Leave
out pairs as shown in the diagram and finish off the motif
with the grey metallic plait.

Point 4:
For the first plait closest to the main motif, add two pairs
of light grass green, and two pairs of medium green for
the plait in the middle. For the last plait add two pairs
of dark green. Add beads at the markings, please see
technique drawing No. 14 on page 9.

Point 5:
The grey metallic plait and the light grass green plait meet
at point 5. Work them together, see technique drawing
No. 7 on page 8.
At pin 1 of the half stitch motif add one Lurex worker,
then six pairs of green, by turns medium green and light
grass green (start with medium green) and work according to the diagram. Leave out pairs as shown.
Finish the two plaits with beads.

Starch the work twice before removing from the lace pillow.

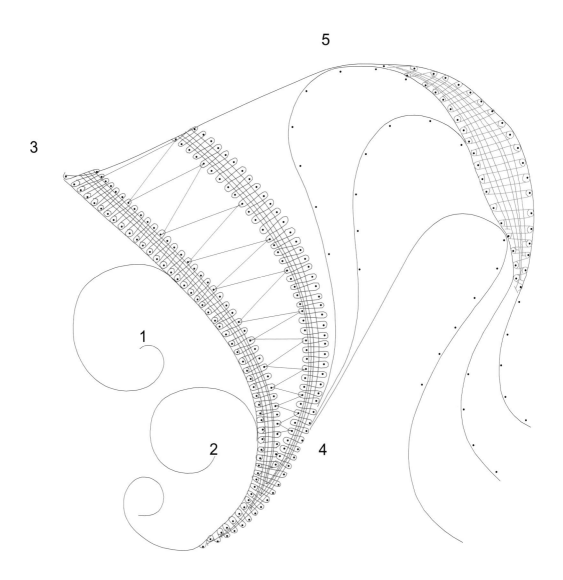

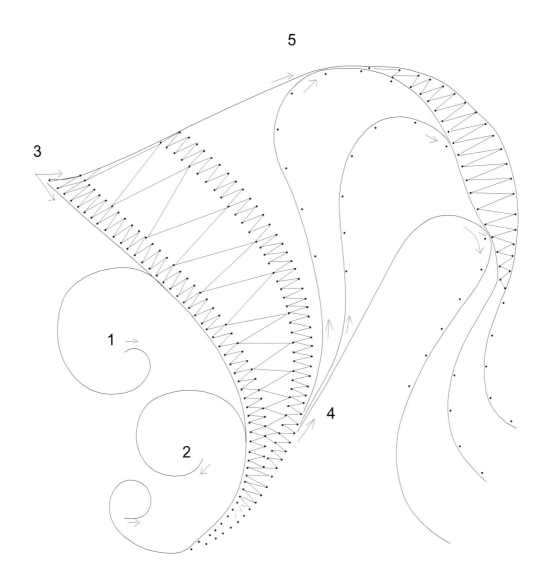

No.12

Threads: Lurex 7005, worker
DMC 5287, grey metallic
Madeira metallic 10-470, peacock green
DMC 701, dark green
Venus 229, medium green
Anchor 240, light grass green
Anchor 259, light loden green

Points A, B, and C:
Start plait A with two pairs of grey metallic and plait B
with two pairs of dark green and plait to the first joining
point. The plaits make a windmill crossing, see technique
drawing No. 9 on page 8. Continue the plaits separately
to the next joining point.
Start plait C with two pairs of grey metallic and plait to
the joining point D. At this point plait A and C make a
windmill crossing and continue with four pairs, please see
technique drawing No. 16 on page 9.

Leaf 1:
Start with one Lurex worker pair on pin 1. Add pairs in
the following colour sequence: one pair of dark green,
two pairs of light loden green, two pairs of medium
green, two pairs of light grass green, and one pair of medium green.
The two pairs of grey metallic continue in a plait down
the middle of the leaf.
Leave out pairs according to the diagram.

Leaf 2:
Turn to begin leaf 2. The two dark green pairs from the
plait become passive pairs. The grey metallic plait continues as plait along the right hand side.
Make a sewing into the lower edge bar of leaf 1, see
technique drawing No. 11 on page 8.
Add pairs in the following colour sequence: one pair of
light grass green, two pairs of peacock green, one pair of
medium green, two pairs of dark green (dark plait), one
pair of dark green, one pair of medium green, and one
pair of light grass green.
Work according to the diagram and leave pairs out of the
plait.
The edge plaits make a windmill crossing at the end of
the motif and the plaits continue (E).

Starch the work twice before removing from the lace pillow.

Diagram

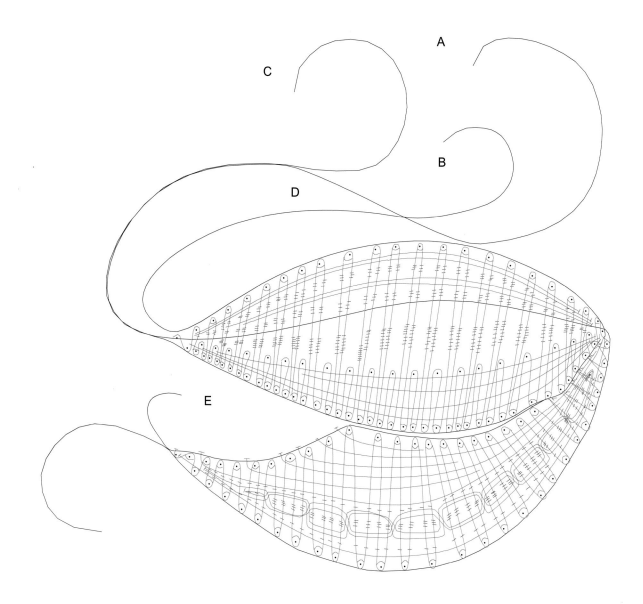

Pricking

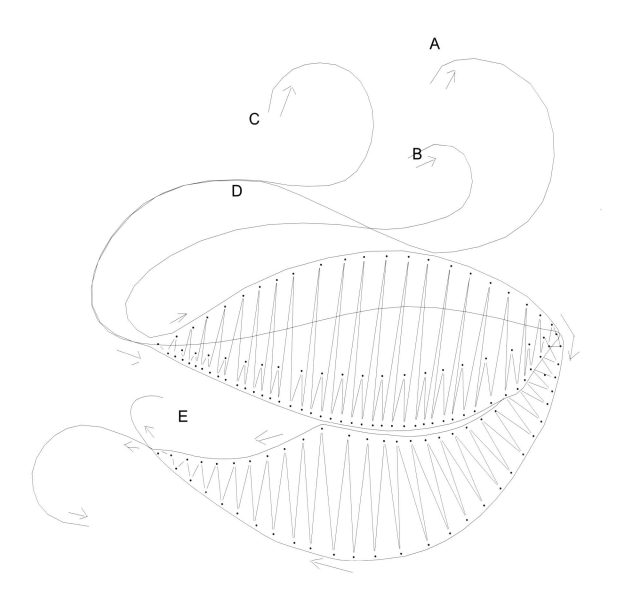

No. 13

Threads: Lurex 7005, worker
DMC 5287, grey metallic
Madeira 327-9810, copper, thick thread
Venus 172, dark orange
Mayflower 1120, orange
Venus 170, light orange
Venus 502, yellow
Venus 542, light yellow

Fig. 1:
Start at point A with one pair of grey metallic and one pair of copper (divided into two). Plait to point B. On pin 1 add two pairs of grey metallic for the right edge plait and one Lurex worker.
Add pairs in the edge plait across the motif in the following colour sequence: one pair of dark orange, one pair of copper, one pair of dark orange, one pair of copper, two pairs of dark orange, one pair of copper, four pairs of orange, five pairs of light orange, and two pairs of grey metallic (left edge plait). Continue according to the diagram. Use supporting pins for the copper threads each time they make a turn.
After working a few rows, remove the supporting pins and pull the copper threads into a soft curve.

Fig. 2:
Start at point B. Add one pair of grey metallic and one pair of copper (divided into two) and plait to the start of fig. 2. The plait is used as the edge plait across the motif, add pairs in the following colour sequence: two pairs of grey metallic for the left hand side edge plait, two pairs of dark orange, two pairs of orange for the chain stitch gimp, (see technique drawing No. 1 on page 7), consisting of one pair of copper and one pair of double dark orange, one pair of light orange, one pair of yellow, one pair of light yellow, one pair of yellow, one pair of light orange for the chain stitch gimp, two pairs of orange, two pairs of dark orange, and two pairs of grey metallic (edge plait for the right hand side).
On pin 2 on the right hand side add one Lurex worker and work according to the diagram.
The two coloured plaits across the motif continue to fig. 3.

Fig. 3:
The two coloured plaits from fig. 2 continue across fig. 3 and end up in a "curl" on the right hand side of the motif. In the plait add pairs in the following colour sequence from the left: two pairs of grey metallic, one pair of light yellow, two pairs of yellow, two pairs of light orange, four pairs of orange, five pairs of dark orange, one pair of copper, two pairs of grey metallic (for the right hand edge plait).
On pin 2 to the left add one Lurex worker, and work according to the diagram.
Finish the work by letting the two pairs of grey metallic continue in a plait, which meet the two coloured plaits from fig. 1. Finish off the two plaits by working seven buttonhole stitches.
After starching the work to the point where five buttonhole stitches remain, cut off.

Starch the work twice before removing from the lace pillow.

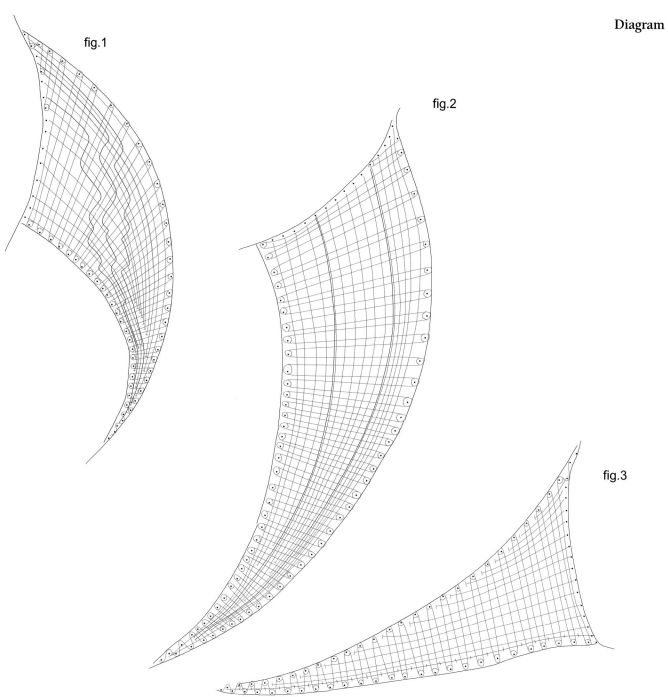

fig.1

fig.2

fig.3

Pricking

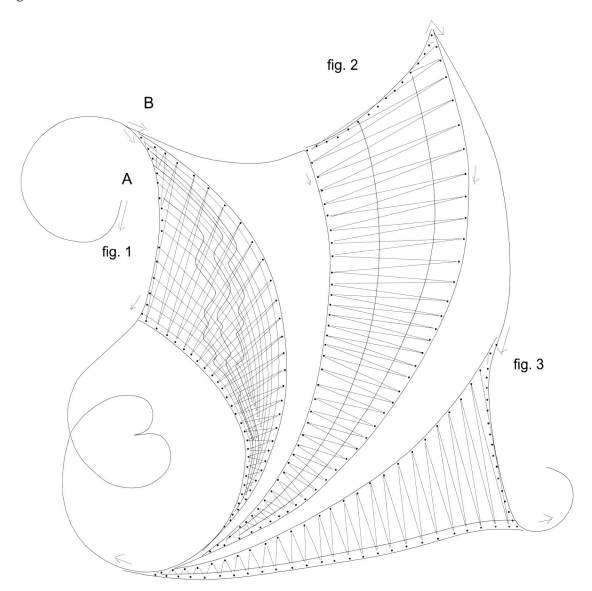

B

A

fig. 2

fig. 1

fig. 3

No. 14

Threads: Lurex 7005, worker
DMC 5287, grey metallic
Madeira 327-9810, copper
Venus 172, dark orange
Mayflower 1120, orange
Venus 170, light orange
Venus 542, light yellow

Fig. 1:
Start with four pairs of grey metallic for plaits on the left
and right hand sides. On pin 1 add one Lurex worker.
Work according to the diagram and add pairs in the following colour sequence from point A to B: four pairs of
dark orange, two pairs of copper, three pairs of orange,
three pairs of light orange, and three pairs of light yellow.
Work according to the diagram to point D. For instruc-
tions how to cross plaits, see technique drawing No. 10
on page 8.

Fig. 2:
After the edge plaits cross, a copper pair and worker pair
are added according to the diagram.
Add pairs at the right hand side of the copper pair, in the
following colour sequence: three pairs of light yellow, two
pairs of light orange, two pairs of orange, and two pairs of
dark orange.
The right hand side edge plait turns and works along the
end of the motif.
Finish off the pairs in the edge plait.
The plait continues according to the arrows on the diagram.
The left hand side edge plait continues to point A, is
sewn in and works back to fig. 2, where it is fastened off.

Fig. 3:
Point B:
Add two pairs of grey metallic to the edge plait and plait
to point C, where two pairs of grey metallic are added.
There are now edge plaits on both sides of the motif. On
pin 1 add one Lurex worker. Add pairs according to the
diagram in the following colour sequence: three pairs of
dark orange, three pairs of orange, and two pairs of light
orange. The motif is worked in half stitch.
Sew in the right hand side edge plait to fig. 1, the edge
plait turns and follows the end of the motif.
Finish off the pairs from the motif in the edge plait.
Where the two edge plaits meet, put in a pin, leave aside
the two middle pairs and continue plaiting using the
outer right and left hand pairs. Finish off the pairs, which
have been left aside.

Fig. 4:
Point E:
Start plaiting with one pair of grey metallic and one pair
of copper (divided into two).
Where the two plaits meet, work a windmill crossing,
see technique drawing No. 9 on page 8. Add one pair of
Lurex for the worker and two pairs of copper. Work ac-
cording to the diagram.

Starch the work twice before removing from the lace pillow.

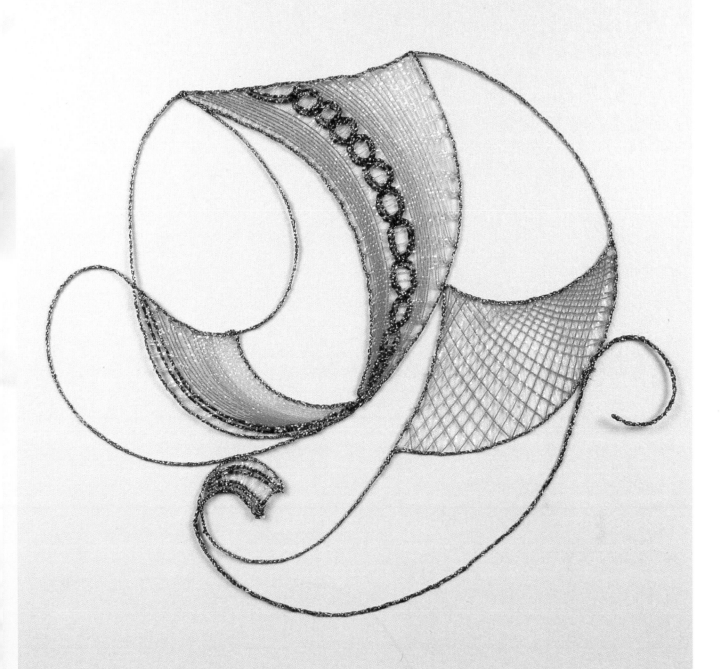

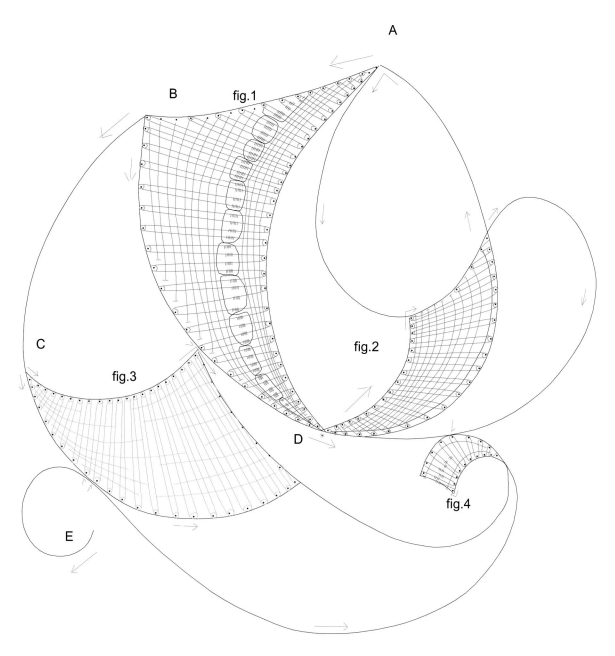

A

B   fig.1

fig.2

C

fig.3

D

fig.4

E

Pricking

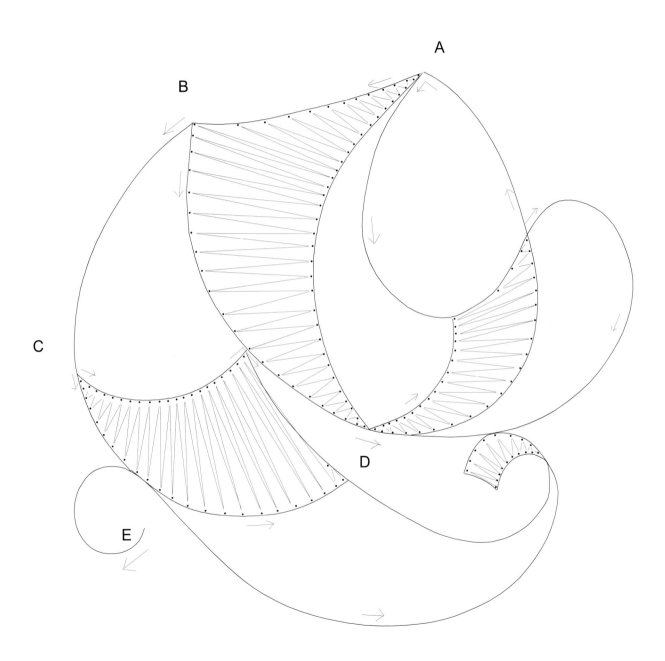

No. 15

Threads: Lurex 7005, worker
DMC 5287, grey metallic
Madeira 327-9810, copper – thick thread
Venus 502, yellow
Venus 542, light yellow
Venus 172, dark orange
Mayflower 1120, orange
Venus 170, light orange

Fig. 1:
Point A:
Start on the left hand side of fig. 1. On pin 1 add four pairs of grey metallic for edge plaits on respectively on the right and left hand sides and one Lurex worker.
Add pairs to the plait across the motif in the following colour sequence: one pair of copper, three pairs of light yellow, two pairs of yellow, two pairs of light orange, two pairs of orange, and one pair of copper.
Point B:
Add two pairs of grey metallic and plait to fig. 1. Work a windmill crossing with the pairs from the two plaits, see technique drawing No. 9 on page 8. The two pairs closest to fig. 1 continue as the edge plait. The other two pairs continue as a plait to fig. 3. Leave aside the pairs. Continue fig. 1 to the tip according to the diagram.
Please see technique drawing No. 10 on page 8, in order to get from fig. 1 to fig. 2 with the four pairs from the plaits, one copper pair and the Lurex worker.

Fig. 2:
Work according to the diagram and add one pair of dark orange at the point shown. Finish off with plaits.
The plaits, which are added half way down fig. 2, are one pair of grey metallic and one pair of copper (divided into two).

Fig. 3:
Plait to pin 1. Add two pairs of grey metallic for a plait and one Lurex worker. Add four pairs of dark orange at the markings in the diagram.
At the markings in the middle of the motif add in pairs open in the following colour sequence: one pair of orange, one pair of light orange, one pair of yellow, and one pair of light yellow. The pairs are finished off in the plait as shown in the diagram.

Starch the work twice before removing from the lace pillow.

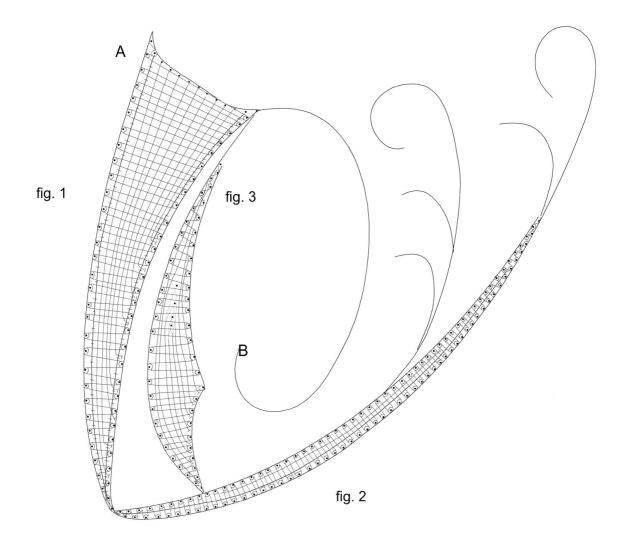

A

fig. 1

fig. 3

B

fig. 2

C

Pricking

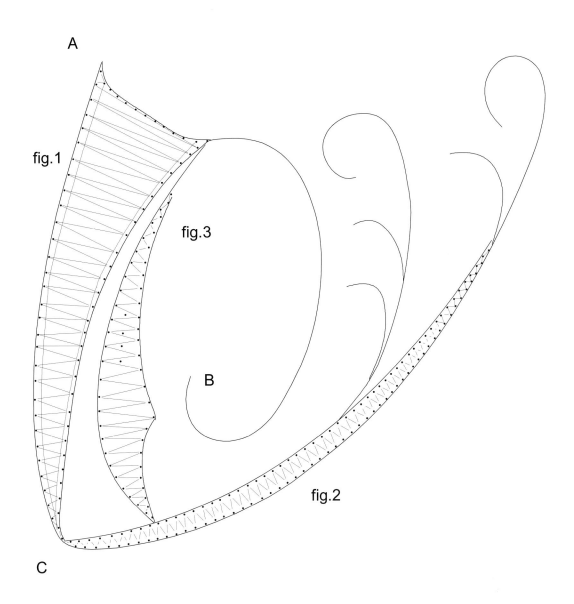

A

fig.1

fig.3

B

fig.2

C

No. 16

Threads: Lurex 7005, worker
DMC 5287, grey metallic
DMC 274, antique silver
Anchor 301 – 2-strands (silver1)
DMC 5283 – 1-strand, metallic silver (silver2)
Madeira 360-2, 2-strands, glossy grey

Point A:
Start with two pairs of grey metallic for the plait and follow the diagram. Add two extra pairs of grey metallic for the second plait.

Fig. 1:
The grey metallic plait continues across the motif, and pairs are added to this plait in the following colour sequence: 2 × 2 pairs of grey metallic for two plaits, one Lurex worker, three pairs of silver1, one pair of grey metallic, three pairs of silver1, one pair of grey metallic, and five pairs of silver1.
Where the two grey metallic passives reach the lower edge, one new pair of grey metallic is added onto each one, and they will now become plaits.

Fig. 2:
At point D start with two pairs of grey metallic for the plait and follow the diagram to point E. Add two extra pairs of grey metallic for the right hand side edge plait. Add one Lurex worker and five pairs of silver2. Work according to the diagram. At point B add two pairs of grey metallic. Plait to fig. 3 and leave the plaits aside. At the end of fig. 2 finish off the five silver pairs and the left hand side plait.

Where the right hand side edge plait meets the first plait from fig. 1, work a windmill crossing and the worker goes through as a passive. See technique drawing No. 9 on page 8.

Fig. 3:
Add pairs to the plait in the following colour sequence: one pair of antique silver, four pairs of glossy grey, and one pair of antique silver. Follow the diagram, and add two pairs of grey metallic to the plaits as indicated. Work all the plaits to point D. Sew into the plait next to the plait starting at point D. Make a Duchesse roll, see technique drawing No. 3 on page 7. When the roll meets fig. 1 sew the roll into the plait and fasten off.

Starch the work twice before removing from the lace pillow.

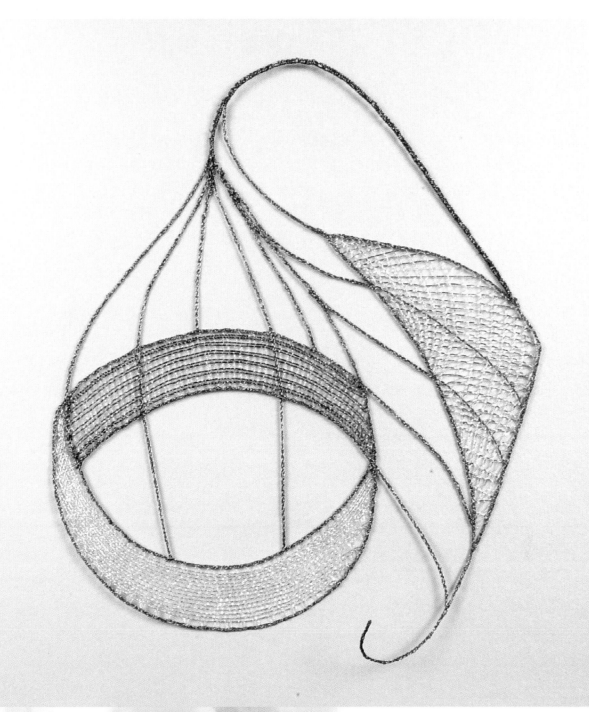

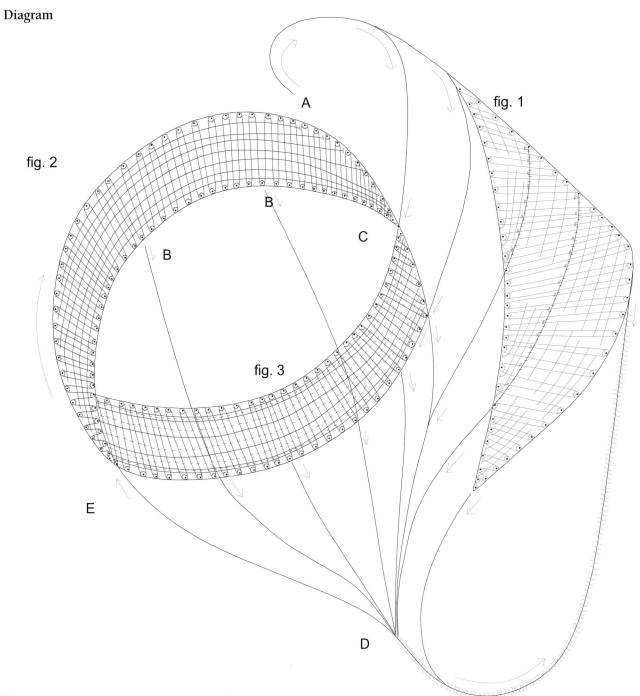

fig. 1

fig. 2

A

B

B

C

fig. 3

E

D

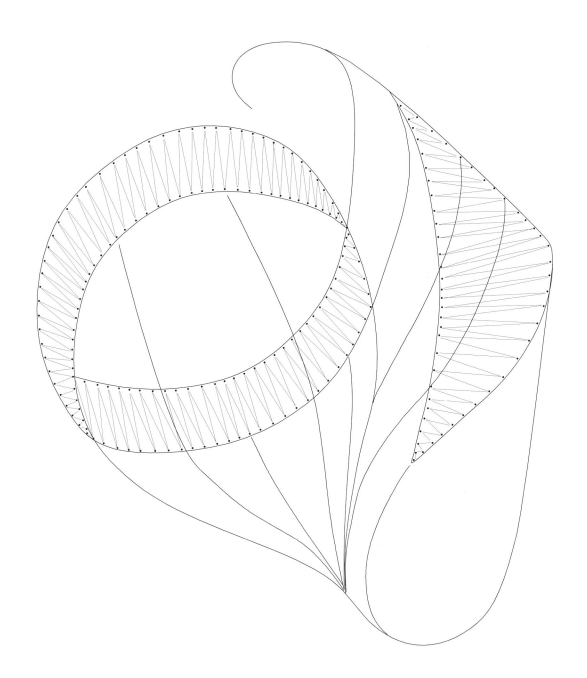

No. 17

Threads: Madeira metallic silver No. 40, thin thread
Madeira metallic silver No. 6, glossy thick thread
Madeira metallic silver No. 12, dull 3-strands
Madeira metallic alu No. 40 (use double thread on each bobbin).
Beads: 2 mm

Fig 1:
Point A:
Add four pairs of silver No. 12 for plaits to go on the right and left hand sides of the motif.
On pin 1 add two pairs of silver No. 40 = two pairs of workers. Add one pair of silver No. 6 and one pair of alu No. 40 as shown on the diagram.
The first time the two workers meet, add a bead. See technique drawing No. 13 on page 9.
Repeat every time the workers meet.
Add pairs according to the diagram: one pair of silver No. 6 (at the left hand side of the work), two pairs of alu No. 40 (right hand side). There are now three pairs of alu No. 40 on the right hand side and three pairs of silver No. 6 on the left hand side. Add extra pairs on the left hand side according to the diagram. Leave out pairs as shown.
Point B:
Work a windmill crossing, see technique drawing No. 9 on page 8, and continue with a Venetian plait to fig. 2, see technique drawing No. 5 on page 7.

Fig. 2:
Divide the pairs and use them for edge plaits on each side of the motif. Add ten pairs of silver No. 40 into the plait across the motif as shown in the diagram. Work in half stitch and leave pairs out of the plait as shown on the diagram.
Point A:
Sew in fig. 1 and 2. The plaits continues as edge plaits in fig. 3.

Fig. 3:
On pin 1 add one pair of silver No. 40 as the worker, and at the markings on the diagram add four pairs of silver No. 6. On the first four pins in the middle of the motif add two pairs at a time in the following colour sequence: two pairs of alu No. 40, and two pairs of alu No. 40, two pairs of silver No. 12, and two pairs of silver No. 12.
On the last pin, according to the diagram, add one pair of silver No. 40, which will be used later as worker for the left hand side of the motif. Work according to the diagram to point C, sew in fig. 2 and 3 and continue according to the diagram to point D.
Point D:
Turn the plait and let it continue across the motif. Sew into the plait at each pin.
At the point where the plaits meet work a windmill crossing, see technique drawing No. 9 on page 8. Now the plaits continue in two directions towards point B. Sew in the plait when it reaches point D. Sew in the plaits when they reach point B and finish off.

Metallic threads are not easy to starch, but to keep knots etc. in shape, the work still has to be starched twice before removing from the lace pillow.

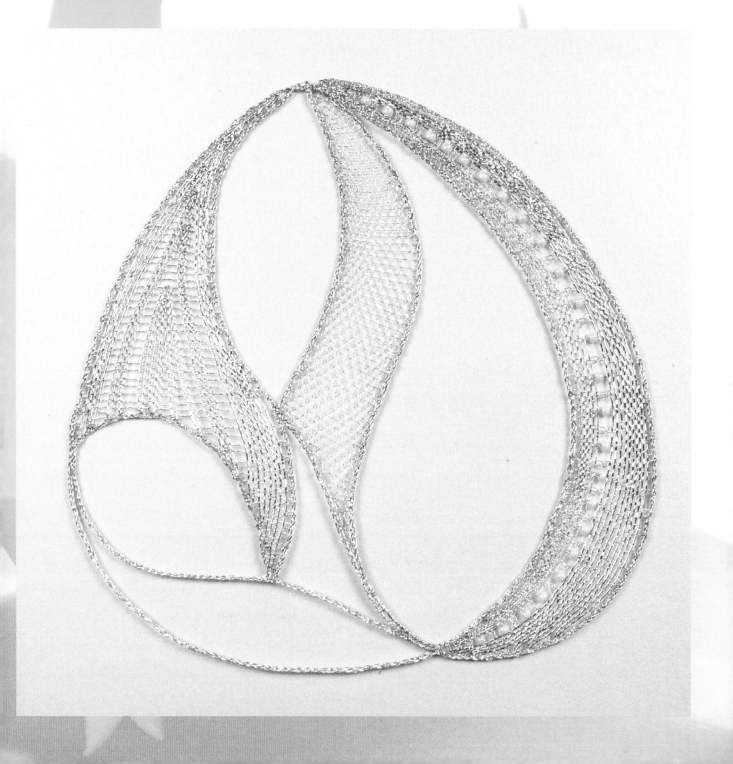

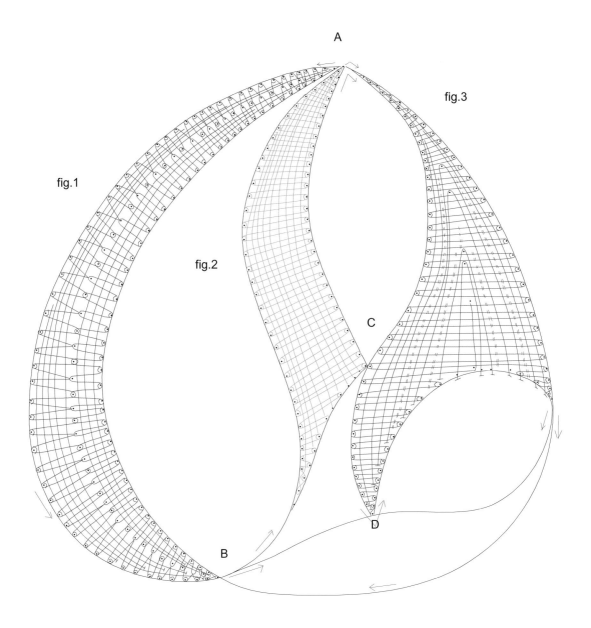

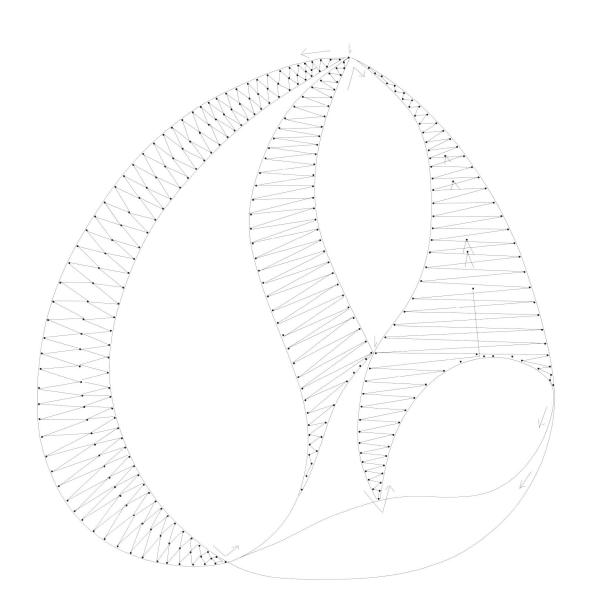

No. 18

Threads: Madeira metallic gold 33 No. 12 – 3-strands (gold1)
Madeira metallic gold 43 No. 6, thick gold thread (gold2)
Madeira metallic gold 6 No. 40, thin gold thread (gold3)
Madeira metallic col. 24 No. 40, thin gold thread (gold4)
Mayflower 4001, gold 6-strands – gimp (gold5)
Mayflower 3999, gold/silver, (gold6)
Anchor 303, medium citrus, use 2 of the 12 strands per bobbin (gold7)

Fig. 1:
Add four pairs of gold1 for the edge plaits. Work according to the diagram and add one worker, gold4, and six pairs of gold5. Work according to the diagram and leave out pairs as shown. Where the two edge plaits meet at point A, work a windmill crossing, see technique drawing No. 9 on page 8. Add a supporting pin close to the last stitch. Fasten off the two middle pairs and leave the other two pairs aside.

Fig.2:
Add four pairs of gold1 for the edge plaits, for the right and left hand sides of the motif. As shown in the diagram add two pairs of gold2, as passive/whole stitch pairs six pairs of gold3. Work according to the diagram and leave pairs out as shown. Where the two edge plaits meet at point A, work a windmill crossing. Add a supporting pin close to the stitch, finish off the two pairs in the middle and put aside the last two pairs.

Fig. 3:
Add four pairs gold1 for edge plaits, for the right and left hand sides of the motif. Work according to the diagram and add one worker, gold3, and six pairs of gold7. Work according to the diagram and leave out the pairs as shown. Where the two edge plaits meet at point A, work a windmill crossing. Add a supporting pin close to the stitch, fasten off the two pairs in the middle and leave the last two pairs aside.

Point A:
Divide the 12 threads into four bundles and make a Venetian plait, see technique drawing No. 5 on page 7. Keep the work as tight as possible.

Fig. 4:
Add four pairs of gold1 for edge plaits, for the right and left hand sides of the motif. Make sure that you have sufficient thread to carry in the plaits for fig. 5 as well. According to the diagram add one worker, gold4. On pin 3 add the gimp pair; all six threads are used. Make sure that you have sufficient thread, as the gimp is divided into single threads and continues in Torchon ground (half stitch) in fig. 5. According to the diagram add nine pairs of gold6, one thread on each bobbin. Work according to the diagram to point B.

Point B:
Leave out the worker. Work a windmill crossing and leave the gimp thread as a bundle to go as passive through the stitch, see technique drawing No. 9 on page 8.

Fig. 5:
The edge plaits from fig. 4 continues as edge plaits in fig. 5. According to the diagram, two threads = one pair from the bundle (the gimp), works in as Torchon ground (half stitch). In this way the gimp disappears into Torchon ground (half stitch). Continue according to the diagram to the tip of the leaf.

Metallic threads are not easy to starch, but to keep knots etc. in shape, the work still has to be starched twice before removing from the lace pillow.

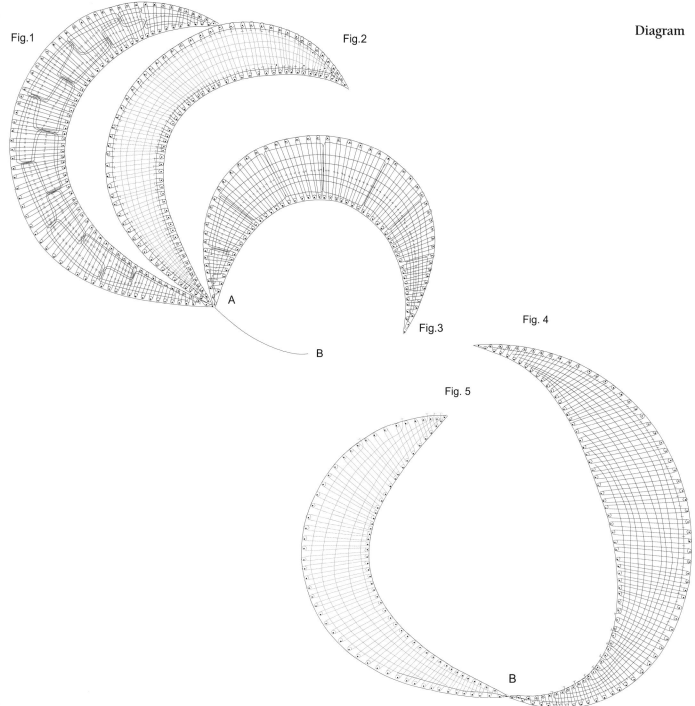

Fig.1

Fig.2

Diagram

A

B

Fig.3

Fig. 4

Fig. 5

B

82

Pricking

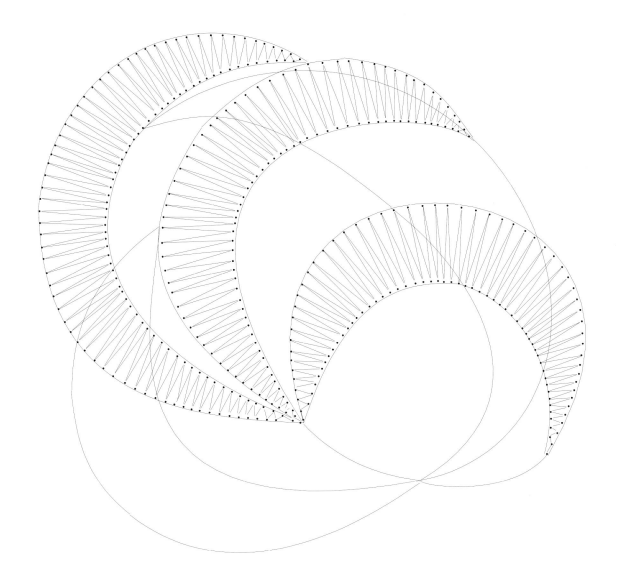

Pricking

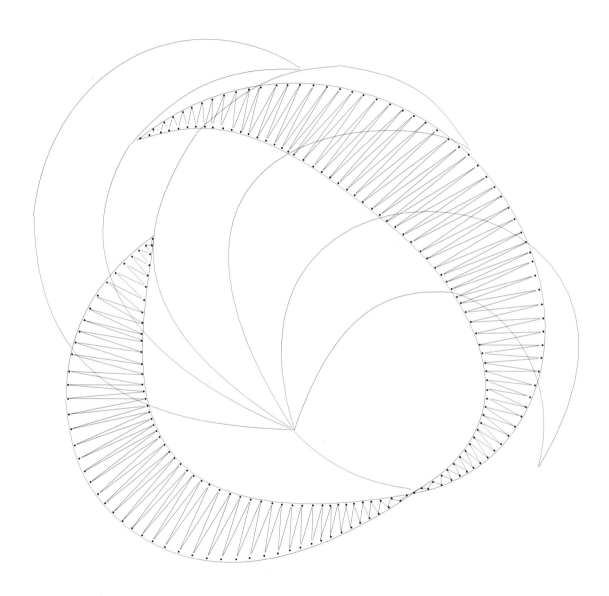